To:_____

From:_____

FATHERS AND SONS

Why Sons Always Need Their Fathers

Written by Meredith R. Katz

new seasons®

A SON NEEDS A FATHER...

...who will assure him that the only shoes
he needs to fill are his own.

...to teach him all of his best moves.

A son needs a father...

...so he knows where to lean
when he needs support.

A SON NEEDS A FATHER...

...to share his sense of adventure.

A SON NEEDS A FATHER...

...to teach him when to lead
and when to follow.

A SON NEEDS A FATHER...

...who believes that time spent with
his children is the best retreat.

A SON NEEDS A FATHER...

...who is a lifelong friend.

A SON NEEDS A FATHER...

...who can make his mood soar.

A SON NEEDS A FATHER...

...whose values make him the
man he aspires to be.

A SON NEEDS A FATHER...

...who treasures every opportunity
to watch him explore.

A SON NEEDS A FATHER...

...to teach him the mechanics of life.

A SON NEEDS A FATHER...

...who will make sure he can take care of himself.

A SON NEEDS A FATHER...

...to teach him what it means to be a brother.

A SON NEEDS A FATHER...

...who is still a kid at heart.

A SON NEEDS A FATHER...

...to help him embrace his heritage.

A SON NEEDS A FATHER...

...to show him that with practice,
anything is attainable.

A SON NEEDS A FATHER...

...to guide him on his path to manhood.

A SON NEEDS A FATHER...

...who will keep him protected —
no matter where he is.

A SON NEEDS A FATHER...

...to make sure he strives for the top.

A SON NEEDS A FATHER...

…who considers his family to be
his most precious gift.

A SON NEEDS A FATHER...

...to show him a place where
he will always belong.

A SON NEEDS A FATHER...

...who shares the sources of his
inspiration with him.

A SON NEEDS A FATHER...

...who would rather spend game day with
him more than anyone else.

A SON NEEDS A FATHER...

...to show him the true meaning of teamwork.

A SON NEEDS A FATHER...

...who welcomes any question
on his road of discovery.

A SON NEEDS A FATHER...

...who is always glad to have him home.

A SON NEEDS A FATHER...

...who makes him feel like he's number one.

…who never hesitates to remind him
where he gets his good looks.

A SON NEEDS A FATHER...

...to teach him that it takes a few misses
to get the perfect swing.

A SON NEEDS A FATHER...

...to be his anchor.

A SON NEEDS A FATHER...

...who has a dynamic spirit.

A SON NEEDS A FATHER...

...who gives him comfort that no one else can.

A SON NEEDS A FATHER...

...who will encourage his spirit
every step of the way.

A SON NEEDS A FATHER...

...to show him the importance
of educating one another.

A SON NEEDS A FATHER...

...who keeps his heart light.

A SON NEEDS A FATHER...

...who is happy to make the journey with him.

Maya Angelou

Maya Angelou

JOURNEY OF THE HEART

Jayne Pettit

A RAINBOW BIOGRAPHY

Lodestar Books

Dutton • New York

Copyright © 1996 by Jayne Pettit

Library of Congress Cataloging-in-Publication Data

Pettit, Jayne.
    Maya Angelou: Journey of the heart / Jayne Pettit.
        p.   cm.—(A Rainbow biography)
    Includes bibliographical references and index.
    Summary: Traces the journey of this Afro-American woman from childhood through her life as an entertainer, civil rights activist, writer, poet, and university professor.
    ISBN 0-525-67518-3 (alk. paper)
    1. Angelou, Maya—Biography—Juvenile literature. 2. Afro-American women authors—20th century—Biography—Juvenile literature. 3. Civil rights workers—United States—Biography—Juvenile literature. 4. Afro-American entertainers—Biography—Juvenile literature. [1. Angelou, Maya. 2. Authors, American. 3. Afro-Americans—Biography. 4. Women—Biography.]   I. Title.   II. Series.
PS3551.N464Z82   1996
818'.5409—dc20
[B]   95-9352
                                                                CIP
                                                                 AC

Published in the United States by Lodestar Books,
an affiliate of Dutton Children's Books,
a division of Penguin Books USA Inc.,
375 Hudson Street, New York, New York 10014

Published simultaneously in Canada
by McClelland & Stewart, Toronto

Editor: Virginia Buckley   Designer: Marilyn Granald

Printed in the U.S.A.   First Edition
10 9 8 7 6 5 4 3 2

to my husband, Bin, and to our children,
Robin, Susan, Bruce, Paul, and Patrick

Contents

A 4-page gallery of photographs appears following page 34.

Acknowledgments

I am deeply grateful to Virginia Buckley, my editor at Lodestar Books, for her wise encouragement and generous assistance during the writing of *Maya Angelou: Journey of the Heart*. Throughout the months spent in research, Virginia's suggestions enabled me to bring into focus the essence of a remarkable and very courageous woman. Special thanks to Barrie Van Dyck, Mary Hardy, and others for their support, and to my husband, Bin, who agreed that Maya Angelou's story should be shared with young readers everywhere.

1

"On the Pulse of Morning"

On a beautiful, sunny day in January of 1993, Maya Angelou—poet, writer, teacher, and lecturer—took her place at the podium on the steps of the Capitol Building in Washington, D.C. Minutes before, William H. Rehnquist, chief justice of the United States Supreme Court, had issued the oath of office to the nation's forty-second president, William Jefferson Clinton.[1]

Dressed in a heavy winter coat to protect her arthritic body from the cold, Dr. Angelou rested her long, slender fingers at the edges of the paper on which she had written her inaugural poem, "On the Pulse of Morning." Before her were throngs of people who had gathered for the ceremony, and beside her on the platform sat a host of dignitaries, including outgoing President George Bush and his wife, Vice President Albert Gore and his family, Supreme Court justices, and members of Congress.

Pausing for a moment, the tall, dignified woman

looked beyond the crowd standing beneath the flag-draped rostrum, and rested her eyes upon the gleaming white marble of the Washington Monument.

For weeks, Maya Angelou had been preparing herself for this occasion, rising before dawn each morning as she frequently did and studying the words of Frederick Douglass, Patrick Henry, and Thomas Paine, three of her favorite people in American history. Pacing slowly back and forth across the floor of her bedroom, she read to herself, drawing inspiration from the words that had moved the nation in times of great turmoil, crisis, or war.

Now, as the hushed crowd waited, Maya Angelou leaned slightly toward the microphone, took a deep breath, and began her poem. Speaking in a voice that rose and fell in harmony with each new line, she wrapped her soft, silken tones around each word, holding her listeners' attention with grace and ease. As always, Maya Angelou's message was one of hope, a promise of a fresh beginning for America and the world.

Later, after the inauguration ceremonies had concluded, Dr. Angelou was the guest of honor at a reception and luncheon held in a lovely restaurant overlooking the Potomac River. Many well-known people from the government and the arts gathered together to meet her and to pay their respects to the woman whose books, plays, and television documentaries had entertained and inspired them. The air was festive and full of the excitement of Inauguration Day, with all of the accompanying ceremonies that take place when the nation's capital celebrates the election of the president.

Maya Angelou's journey to Washington and to the steps of the Capitol had been long and difficult. But, despite its painful beginnings so many years before, it was a remarkable journey of a woman whose courage, faith, and determination had given her the strength to conquer her innermost fears in the face of overwhelming odds.

2
The Train to Somewhere

Three-year-old Marguerite Johnson held her brother's hand tightly as they watched the train chug its way slowly into the Long Beach, California, station. On the platform, groups of people were hugging one another and saying their good-byes. Stacks of suitcases, cloth satchels, and cardboard boxes tied with cord lined the station, and somewhere nearby, a baby cried.

Bailey, one year older than Marguerite, felt for the tickets that were pinned to the inside of his coat pocket. On his wrist was the same tag as the one his sister wore: "To whom it may concern, in care of Mrs. Annie Henderson, Stamps, Arkansas."[2]

The children's father, a big man with a ready smile and laughing eyes, called to a porter, asking him to look after his children on their long journey. Then, hurrying them along, he waved as the little boy and girl followed the man up the train steps and into the dusty railroad car.

On the following day in Arizona, the porter who had been in charge of Marguerite and Bailey got off the train. Alone and frightened, the two children stared out the window, saying little to each other as the hours and the days dragged slowly by.

When they reached the South, a number of other Negro[3] passengers, feeling sorry for Marguerite and Bailey, gave them food from their lunch boxes. (In the segregated southern states, blacks were not permitted to eat in the dining car with whites.) But despite these kindnesses, the little boy and girl could not fight off their confusion about what was happening to them. Why had their parents decided to get a divorce and why were they sending their children so far away from home?

In 1930, Stamps, Arkansas, was a musty, rural town of fewer than twenty-five hundred people. Less than forty miles from the Louisiana border, it was deep in the heart of the Cotton Belt. An invisible line divided one section of town from the other. Poor back-country whites lived on one side and even poorer blacks lived on the other. A scattering of small shops and houses lined the main street of the white part of town. In the black section, a dirt road led to the Wm. Johnson General Merchandise Store.

The owner of the store was Mrs. Annie Henderson, mother of William and Bailey Johnson Sr. More than twenty-five years earlier, when Annie found herself with two small babies to feed after the breakup of her first marriage, she set up a small, wooden stand between the old cotton mill and the lumber mill. There she sold homemade meat pies for a nickel each.

"I looked up the road I was going and back the way I come, and since I wasn't satisfied, I decided to step off the road and cut me a new path," Annie once said.[4]

In time, Annie Henderson's long hours of hard work paid off, and the tiny lunch stand grew into the store that bore the name of her crippled son, Willie. It was here that she took in her son Bailey's children, Marguerite and Bailey Johnson Jr.

Annie Henderson's store, in the heart of the Negro section of Stamps, was the center of all activity. On Saturdays, its front porch turned into a barbershop, and traveling hoboes would stop to rest and receive food from Annie. In return, the men would sing old songs for her, plunking away on their handmade musical instruments. Inside the store, customers could find coal oil for their lamps, lightbulbs if they had electricity, and food for themselves and their animals. If a customer asked for something Annie didn't have, she'd get it from somewhere.

To Marguerite and Bailey, Grandmother Annie was an immediate source of comfort and stability. A tall woman with boundless energy and hands made rough from years of hard work, she awakened each morning before dawn and got down on her knees to thank the Lord for bringing her safely through the night. To the members of her church and to everyone in this part of town, "Sister Henderson" was a tower of strength and an angel of hope.

Soon after their arrival in Stamps, the two children settled into Annie's routine. Time passed quickly as they went about their chores, and it was not long before a close bond of security, warmth, and love developed among Maya (her brother's name for her), Bailey, and the woman they had begun to call Momma.

When Maya and her brother were old enough to attend school, they rose at dawn and scrubbed themselves at the outdoor pump and dressed in fresh clothing laid out by Momma. After a hearty breakfast, they helped out in the store, scooping flour into thin paper sacks and filling the onion and potato bins, before walking to school. On summer days when school was out, they helped Momma with the customers and fed the hogs and the chickens. Sundays were spent in church, where they sat for hours with Momma while the preacher delivered his sermons, and rocked and swayed to the sounds of the gospel chorus.

Under the strict guidance of Momma and Uncle Willie, Maya and her brother became excellent students in school. From the experience they gained by working in the store, arithmetic came easily to them. Reading was a favorite pastime, and they devoured books by the dozens. At an unusually early age, the two children were reading Shakespeare to each other.

One evening, while Maya and Bailey were feeding the hogs, a man who had once been the town sheriff rode up to the store. Easing himself off his horse with an air of authority, he strode through the front door.

"Annie, tell Willie he better lay low tonight. A crazy nigger messed with a white lady today. Some of the boys'll be coming over here later."[5]

The two children, who had come running at the sound of horse's hooves on the dusty road, watched in silence as the man rushed from the store and galloped away.

The "boys," as Maya and Bailey knew, were members of the local Ku Klux Klan, an organization of hate-filled white men who terrorized and lynched blacks throughout the South.

Going into the store, the children saw Momma blowing out the coal-oil lamps. Then, after speaking to Uncle Willie in a low voice, Momma ordered the children to take the potatoes and onions out of their bins and to knock out the walls dividing them.

Hurrying down the aisle as quickly as his twisted body would allow, Uncle Willie handed his cane to Maya and bent down to climb painfully into the empty bins. The children covered him with the potatoes and onions while Momma knelt, praying in the pitch-black darkness of the store.

Maya never slept that night. Momma's prayers must have worked, for the white-sheeted Klansmen with their blazing torches never came. But if they had, Uncle Willie's terrible moaning hour after hour would surely have betrayed his hiding place, and one more black man would have been dragged to the lynching tree.

Little Maya adored her handsome brother. It was Bailey to whom she confided her darkest secrets, deepest fears, and worries about her awkwardness. When the neighborhood children tormented her about her big size and hair that stuck out in every direction, Bailey comforted her by saying she was the most beautiful person he'd ever seen. And when relatives made unkind remarks about her features, Bailey always found ways to take revenge.

Maya thought her brother was an absolute whiz at everything. A brilliant child with limitless energy, he finished his chores quickly, and he could read more books and win more games than anyone in the neighborhood. In fact, the shy, lonely little girl thought that her brother was just about perfect.

Each summer, Maya and Bailey helped Momma and the neighborhood women can their vegetables and fruits. After the first frost, they helped the men

9

slaughter the hogs and any of the cows that had stopped giving milk. In the Negro section of Stamps, everyone assisted everyone else.

After the hogs were slaughtered, the missionary ladies of the church would come and make sausages with Momma for the smokehouse, and each of the neighborhood children who had helped load the woodstove would stand in line for mouth-watering samples of the spicy little meats. The men-folk did the heavy work, hauling the big sides of meat to the smokehouse and opening the knuckle of each ham to remove the bone. Then they would rub coarse brown salt into the flesh to bring the blood to the surface.

Momma and her neighbors counted on the smokehouse meats and the harvest from their vegetable gardens to carry them through the winter, and Maya and Bailey would hungrily eye the beautiful home-canned goods on the shelves of the store: green beans and collards and cabbage, tomatoes for buttered biscuits, and berries picked at just the right time.

Annie Henderson lived by twelve commandments. To the ten drawn up by God and Moses, she added her own two: "Thou shalt not be dirty" and "Thou shalt not be impudent."

Every night, even in the coldest winter, Maya and Bailey had to go to the backyard pump to wash themselves thoroughly with ice-cold water from the well. Then, after passing inspection, they would do their homework, have their corn bread and milk, and dash off to their tiny bedroom for the night.

As for impudence, there was none in Momma's home. Grown-ups were addressed as Mister, Missus, Miss, Auntie, Cousin, Uncle, and all of the other titles that showed respect. Momma insisted on that.

But there were times when Momma had to keep her silence, like the hot summer day when a group of white girls who lived on her farmland gathered in front of the store to make fun of her. Maya watched from the screen door while Momma pulled her six foot frame up to its full height, folded her arms across her apron, and stared the girls down. Suddenly, the leader of the group whispered something to the others and everyone ran off. Momma just stood there for a bit, strong and powerful. She had held her ground, and Maya was proud of her.

Each Christmas, separate packages would arrive from California, one from the children's mother and another from their father. And each year, Maya and Bailey would feel the pain of that horrible day at the train station in Long Beach. They hated their presents and would run from the store, sitting alone on the cold, wet ground. Maya would weep silently as if her heart would break and Bailey would sniff and dab at his eyes.

Then, one day, the children's father appeared at

the door. He was even bigger and handsomer than Maya and Bailey had dreamed of in their secret talks. Well dressed and smiling broadly, he stepped out of his highly polished De Soto and came up the steps of the store.

Three weeks later, Maya and Bailey were on their way to St. Louis to live with Grandmother Baxter, their mother's mother. And for the second time in her young life, Maya's world was turning upside down.

3

St. Louis

Maya cried almost all of the way to St. Louis. She felt betrayed by this father-stranger who had come without warning to take her away from Momma.

"I want to go back to Stamps," she had sobbed from the backseat of the car, where she sat wedged between her father's fine leather suitcases and the cardboard boxes that held the children's clothing, books, and journals.

And now, as she and her brother waited for their mother to walk into Grandmother Baxter's living room, she was terrified of the woman who had sent her away nearly five years earlier. She longed for the warmth and security of Momma's loving arms and the feeling that she belonged somewhere. And then, through the door came the most beautiful woman Maya had ever seen. With skin as light as Bailey's and bright red lips that flashed a dazzling

13

smile, Vivian Baxter swept back into Maya's and Bailey's lives as quickly as she had left.

To Maya and Bailey, St. Louis, Missouri, was a world apart from the dusty little town of Stamps, Arkansas. Big, noisy, and cluttered with soot-covered buildings crowded against one another, it was a city of strangers.

The black neighborhood during the 1930s was like a cowboy frontier town with its pool halls, gambling dens, and saloons. On every street corner, men with names like Two Gun, Poker Pete, and Hard-Hitting Johnny stood about aimlessly, looking for the next card game or the newest lottery.

Many of these men, including gamblers, bootleg whiskey salesmen, and numbers runners of the area, were frequent visitors to Grandmother Baxter's house on Caroline Street. When Maya and Bailey returned from school, they often found the men there, waiting quietly for Grandmother Baxter's return. A neighborhood precinct captain, Grandmother was a woman of influence with the St. Louis Police Force. To win her favor as well as her protection, the men had only to show up to vote for her on Election Day. It was Grandmother Baxter who closed or opened the gambling parlors and saloons or got a friend released from the local jails. And it was she, with her tough sons, who could take on the meanest of crooks.

Everything was different in St. Louis. Maya and Bailey had their first jelly beans, salted peanuts, and other delicious nuts they'd never seen. There were sandwiches bulging with lettuce and thinly sliced lunch meats, and Victrola machines that played music, as if by magic, on big black discs that spun around.

The local elementary school looked like a brick fortress with its drab exterior and large concrete playground. Maya and Bailey were far ahead of their classmates in all subjects and quickly moved on to higher grades because of their excellent arithmetic and reading skills.

At first, Maya and Bailey seldom saw their mother, who lived in her own home in another part of the city. Once in a while she would take them to Louie's, a tavern owned by two Syrian brothers. Going in by the back door, they were treated to shrimp and soft drinks and sat in dark wooden booths. Then, while they watched in fascination, Vivian Baxter would dance to the music of a jukebox. With grace and beauty she moved and floated in front of them, swaying to the music as if she were a part of it. And when Vivian Baxter began singing her deep-throated blues songs, all eyes were upon her. It was at Louie's that Maya and Bailey first learned to dance the time step, which is the basis of most African American dances. They became so good that their mother loved showing them off to all of her fun-loving friends, who rewarded them with still more shrimp and soda.

Vivian Baxter's brothers, especially Uncle Tutti,

Uncle Tommy, and Uncle Ira, were well known in the neighborhood. They all had jobs working for the city, and were mean, tough, and full of the Baxter bond of loyalty. A man had to be a fool to cross them in any way.

Uncle Tommy was Maya and Bailey's favorite. They loved his jokes and the handball games he taught them to play on the side of Grandmother Baxter's house. And in spite of his rough talk, he was kind, especially to Maya.

"Ritie," he would say, "don't worry 'cause you ain't pretty. Plenty pretty women I seen diggin' ditches or worse. You smart. I swear to God, I rather you have a good mind."[6]

After six months in the big house with Grandmother Baxter and all of the uncles, Maya and Bailey were sent to live with their mother. For the first time, they each had their own room, a bed with crisp new sheets, plenty to eat (their mother was an excellent cook), and a closet full of new clothes.

Vivian Baxter saw to it that her children had their meals on time, did their homework, said their prayers, and got to bed early. Then she would leave for the taverns and her card games.

The children were not alone in the house. Mr. Freeman, their mother's boyfriend, was always there, sitting in the corner by the radio, his huge frame taking up most of the chair. He seldom talked. Hour after hour, he would sit staring into space, waiting for Vivian's return. A man much older than she, he adored her for her beauty, laughter, and intelligence.

One spring Saturday, several months after Maya and her brother had come to live with their mother, Maya was getting ready to go to the library. Her mother was out, and Bailey had gone to play baseball. As she started for the front door, Mr. Freeman called to her.

"Ritie, come here."

Maya saw the big man sitting in his chair, but as she walked toward him, something made her stop. "No, sir, Mr. Freeman," she said, backing away.

Grabbing Maya, the man turned up the volume of the radio until it was blaring. "Now, this ain't gonna hurt you much . . . if you scream, I'm gonna kill you. And if you tell, I'm gonna kill Bailey."[7]

Much later, after the pain had ripped through her body and blinded her senses, Maya somehow summoned the strength to leave the house. She had to get to Bailey. Not to tell him. She didn't dare, or Mr. Freeman would kill him. Unable to find her brother, the little girl started for home. Mother would be there now, and perhaps Bailey.

With her whole body throbbing, Maya struggled to put one foot in front of the other. One step, two, three. At last she reached home. Peeking into the living room, she found Mr. Freeman's chair empty. Climbing the steps with agonizing slowness, she walked to her bedroom and hid her underclothes under the mattress.

Later, Vivian Baxter returned to find her daughter in bed. Taking her temperature, she thought the child was coming down with the measles that were sweeping through the neighborhood. She left the room to get some hot broth.

Suddenly, Mr. Freeman was standing over Maya's bed. Bending down until his face was close to hers, the man repeated his threat to kill Bailey if she dared to tell him what had happened.

The next morning, Maya awakened to find herself drenched with perspiration. The nightmares that had haunted her ever since her parents' divorce had returned, and her whole body ached. When Maya's mother came to check her temperature, Maya was relieved to learn that Mr. Freeman had packed his belongings and left the house.

Minutes later, Bailey walked into the room, and his mother ordered him to take off the wet sheets and to bring fresh ones. As Bailey did so, Maya's blood-stained underclothes dropped to the floor. In an instant, the child's mother realized what had happened. Maya had been raped.

At the hospital, Maya's room was filled with members of the Baxter family. Her mother brought her flowers and candy, and Grandmother Baxter came with baskets of fruit. All of the uncles were there, too, pacing back and forth and grumbling angrily.

Bailey pleaded with Maya to tell him who had abused her, or another child could be hurt. For a long time, the little girl struggled with Mr. Freeman's threats that he would kill Bailey. Finally, with Bailey sobbing at her bedside, Maya told him her terrible secret.

Soon after that, Mr. Freeman was arrested.

The courtroom was jammed with Grandmother Baxter's people: the gamblers and their women, the numbers runners and the saloon keepers, and of course, all of the uncles.

Maya took the witness stand, pulling her coat around her for comfort. Staring across the room at Mr. Freeman, she remained silent as the man's attorney fired questions at her. All she could think about were the threats upon Bailey's life.

The people in the courtroom rustled in their seats. At last, Maya broke her silence. With her eyes on Mr. Freeman, she screamed out his name.

Later that day, while Maya and Bailey were staying with their grandmother, the doorbell rang. Answering it, Grandmother Baxter faced a policeman standing in the doorway. Mr. Freeman's body had been found in the lot behind the slaughterhouse. He had been kicked to death.

4

Journey out of Silence

In the weeks following the murder, eight-year-old Maya stopped talking to anyone but Bailey. Alone in her silent world and believing that Mr. Freeman's death must have been her fault, she kept to herself, staying away from her playmates and their neighborhood games.

Soon, Maya and Bailey were again living with Grandmother Baxter and the uncles. Annoyed by Maya's strange behavior, her uncles and other relatives thought she was just being rude and took to spanking her for not talking. Finally, not knowing what to do with the child, the family decided to send Maya and Bailey back to Arkansas.

On the long train ride, Bailey cried as if his heart would break. He hadn't wanted to leave St. Louis. Most of all, he hadn't wanted to leave the beautiful woman he had come to call Mother Dear. He would miss her visits to Grandmother Baxter's house and the wonderful presents she always brought. Most of all, he would miss her laughter and fun-loving ways.

Shortly after their return, however, Maya began to grow stronger. She felt safe with Momma and Uncle Willie. Nothing could happen to her in the sleepy little town of Stamps. Nothing ever happened there.

The weeks passed into months, and Maya's days were filled with school activities, homework, and helping Momma in the store. Bailey entertained everyone with his wild stories about life in the big city "up North," and people would crowd around him to ask questions.

Maya and Bailey continued to earn high grades in school. They shared their deepest secrets, read to each other, and waited for summers to arrive with their church picnics and fish fries. Maya especially loved the Sunday revival meetings under the big tents and the gospel songs that seemed to rise up to heaven itself. Although she wouldn't sing or speak to anyone but Bailey, the music filled her with a kind of peace and a feeling that everything would be all right.

Maya did not break her silence for five years. She began to keep journals and to write poetry. In the school library, she discovered Charles Dickens and other great English writers, as well as the works of black poets such as Langston Hughes, Paul Laurence Dunbar, and James Weldon Johnson. Creeping under the empty space beneath the store, she would whisper softly to herself as her eyes moved across the pages.

One warm summer day, as Maya was helping Momma in the store, Mrs. Flowers, a well-educated black woman who was known as the aristocrat of Stamps, walked in. Maya watched admiringly as the woman chose some foods from the shelves. Always dressing well and wearing beautiful hats, she seemed to Maya the most elegant lady in town.

When Maya went to Mrs. Flowers's home with the shopping bags, the woman invited her in for cookies and lemonade. As the two sat together, Mrs. Flowers told Maya that she had heard she was a fine student but that she would not speak in class. Taking a book in her hand, the woman began to read from Dickens's *A Tale of Two Cities*. Maya had already read the story and knew it well, although she didn't understand all of its meaning.

"It was the best of times, it was the worst of times . . ." Mrs. Flowers read in her soft, musical voice as Maya hung on each familiar line. Then, letting the book rest in her lap, the woman told Maya that it took the beauty of the human voice to bring power and richness of expression to the printed word.

Maya and her new friend met frequently after that first wonderful day. In the beginning, Mrs. Flowers would read aloud while Maya listened eagerly. Often, the two would walk to the library and browse through the shelves.

Then one day, as she sat listening to Mrs. Flowers read, Maya did more than listen. She began to speak. After years of talking to no one but Bailey, Maya had broken her silence at last.

In the spring of 1940, Maya graduated from the eighth grade. Second in her class, she shared top honors with classmate Henry Reed. There was so much to look forward to. And in the fall, she would be attending high school with Bailey!

And then one afternoon, something terrible happened. Bailey, after running an errand for Uncle Willie in the white section of town, returned to the store upset and frightened. When Uncle Willie and Momma asked him what was wrong, he just stood by the cash register, shivering. Finally, he spoke.

Crossing the bridge over the pond, Bailey said, he had spotted some men pulling the body of a dead black man out of the water. One of the men saw the boy and told him to run home as fast as he could. Suddenly, a white man appeared on the scene and ordered the men and Bailey to pick up the body and take it to the local jail.

Momma knew what had happened. Another black man had been lynched by a white mob. It wasn't the first lynching Stamps had ever seen and it wouldn't be the last. Bailey was in danger now, that was certain. Momma made up her mind that her grandchildren would be safer in California, where their mother had remarried and was living once again.

5

San Francisco

Maya and Bailey thought that San Francisco was the most beautiful place they had ever seen. Ringed by rolling hills that stretched far beyond the bay, it was a city of many cultures and contrasting worlds. During the Gold Rush of 1848, people had flocked to California to seek their fortune in the gold mines. Later, others followed to build the great rail lines that would connect the East with the West. Chinese, Japanese, Mexicans, and people from all parts of the country and as far away as the British Isles and Europe came to find work and a better way of life.

After the Japanese attack on Pearl Harbor in 1941, a new wave of people began moving into San Francisco. Blacks from the South and elsewhere arrived in great numbers to work in the defense plants and weapons and aircraft factories that shot up quickly in the city and surrounding areas. These workers settled in the sprawling neighborhoods that had been vacated by Japanese Americans, who had been sent into detention camps because the government feared they might be potential spies.

Vivian Baxter, Maya and Bailey's mother was now married to a successful San Francisco business-man, and she happily welcomed her children into her new home and her new life. Her husband, whom the children came to know as Daddy Clidell, was a generous and loving man who quickly became the first real father that Maya and her brother had ever had.

Maya took to the city immediately. She loved all of its wonderful old neighborhoods, the Chinese temples and Japanese pagodas, the women moving gracefully down the streets in their long, narrow kimonos, the open-air markets bursting with brightly colored fruits and vegetables. Looking out across the bay with its magnificent Golden Gate Bridge, she would watch the fog roll in with its cloudlike swirls. Gleaming red cable cars chugged up and down Nob Hill, their bells clanging out the distinctive rhythms that marked each conductor's specialty. San Francisco was indeed a city of wonder and excitement.

Maya soon became an outstanding student at George Washington High School. Once more ahead of her grade, she worked hard at her studies. Her favorite teacher was Miss Kirwin, a remarkable woman who was as strong an influence on Maya's love of learning as Mrs. Flowers had been in

Stamps. Miss Kirwin, who taught civics and current events, challenged her students to think, to read about world happenings, and to discuss them in class. Maya lost no time in getting to know the neighborhood library, for books continued to be her passion. In quiet moments, she worked on her poetry and the journals she had begun to keep so long ago in Stamps.

When Maya was fourteen, she won a scholarship to attend evening classes in drama and dance. After each session, she hurried home to practice her lessons with Bailey. Maya did so well that she was awarded a scholarship for the second year. Soon, she and Bailey were following the Big Band dances that came to town. In an auditorium crowded with servicemen and women, they danced the lindy and the jitterbug and the half-time Texas hop.

But as time passed, Maya began to notice a change in Bailey. Falling in with a rough crowd, he was losing interest in school and staying out past the curfew his mother and Daddy Clidell had set for him. One night, after a bitter argument with his mother, Bailey filled a pillowcase with his clothes and left the house, telling Maya that she could have all of his books.

Maya was shattered. For as long as she could remember, she and Bailey had always been together, sharing their deepest secrets and darkest fears. It was Bailey who had defended her and pro-tected her. Now he was gone.

* * *

After Bailey left home, Maya found it hard to concentrate on her studies. She felt lost and alone and thought about running away. What should she do?

Finally an idea came to her. She would leave school for a semester, get a job, earn some money, and buy some clothes. The change might do her good. Later, when she felt better about things, she would go back to school.

When Maya told her mother that she was going to apply for a job as a cable car conductor, Vivian Baxter reminded her of something she hadn't thought about. The city of San Francisco had never hired a black cable car conductor, although any number of white women had replaced male conductors who had left to join the military.

But Maya was determined to find a way. For weeks, she hounded the city's Negro support organizations, asking for help in getting a cable car job. In the meantime, she made regular visits to the cable car office, waiting for hours to be interviewed.

At last, Maya was rewarded for her efforts. Dressed in a smart blue conductor's uniform and snappy hat, she clung to the back of the trolley as it zoomed up and down the steep hills along Market Street, past rooming houses for soldiers and seamen on leave, and sailed on through the beautiful slopes of Golden Gate Park leading into the Sunset District. For a full school semester, she traveled the only route open to her and during the only hours she could get, the night shift.

Back in school, Maya threw herself into her studies and quickly made up for the lost semester. Life was better now in many ways. Bailey had joined the merchant marine and, after months of silence, had written to her. Maya's world was looking brighter, except that she had never had a date with a boy. She wasn't pretty. She was too shy to flirt. And most of all, she was too tall and skinny!

Then, one evening after she had completed her homework, Maya took a walk and ran into a boy in her class. He was friendly and easygoing. Perhaps because of this, the young girl's shyness left her, and moments later they were walking to a friend's place.

The friend answered the door and asked them in. The next thing Maya knew, he was gone. And she and her classmate were alone.

Months later, Maya received her high school diploma. On graduation night, she sat down to write her parents a note. In it, she apologized for bringing disgrace on the family. Maya was pregnant.

After giving birth to a beautiful baby boy, Maya returned home to the loving support of her mother and Daddy Clidell, who saw to it that she and the little one had everything to make them comfortable. Maya passed her days in total contentment, marveling at each development in her baby's growth: his first smile, his first giggle, his first tooth.

In time, however, Maya became restless. She longed for a home of her own and a chance to be independent. After much thought, she decided that she would find a job and a tiny apartment and hire someone who could take care of baby Guy while she worked.

The year was 1945. World War II had ended, and once again there was hope for humankind. Seventeen-year-old Maya was filled with hope, too.

6

Europe and Beyond

For the next seven years, Maya held a number of different jobs and was proud to be on her own. She cooked and cleaned her tiny apartment and filled every empty space with books and music. On her days off, she and Guy took walks in the park, where they read together and Guy played with other children his age.

In 1952, Maya met a sailor named Tosh Angelos. Like Maya, Tosh loved music, and the two began to see each other frequently. They had picnics in Golden Gate Park, and Tosh taught little Guy to play handball and chess. Soon Maya and Tosh were married and settled into a small house. But the two had little in common, and Maya realized that she had made a mistake in marrying so hastily. Before long, the marriage ended.

Eager to try new things, Maya applied for work as a singer at a popular San Francisco nightclub called the Purple Onion. In a short time, she was writing songs with lyrics from her poems. Once, when Maya forgot the words, she danced around the little stage until the lines came back to her. The audience loved her dancing, and she decided to make it a part of the show. Before long, crowds were lining up outside the club every night waiting to get in.

Many show business celebrities began coming to the Purple Onion to see Maya perform. One evening, a group of singers and dancers from a touring company of *Porgy and Bess* were in the audience, and they asked Maya to join them after the show. The next night, the producer of the opera came to the Purple Onion with his wife and several others. At the end of Maya's performance, the producer introduced himself and told her that the company would soon have an opening for a dancer who could also sing.

Maya knew that this was a wonderful opportunity and agreed to audition during one of the rehearsals. Three days later, she was offered the job as the principal dancer in *Porgy and Bess*. But she had to turn down the offer because the Purple Onion had just extended her contract for two months.

Then, three days before her contract was to end, she received a call from the producer of a new Broadway play, *House of Flowers,* starring Pearl Bailey. Could she come to New York to audition for a part in the musical?

Happy for the opportunity, Maya hastily made

arrangements to leave Guy in the care of her mother and flew to New York. On the day after the audition, while Maya waited anxiously in her hotel room, a note was delivered to her door addressed to Maya Angelou, the name she had adopted after her divorce from Tosh Angelos. She had won the part!

Minutes later, the telephone rang, and Maya could hardly believe what was happening. The caller was Bob Dustin, the producer of *Porgy and Bess*, asking her to come to Montreal to begin rehearsals for the dance lead. The company was giving its last performances before leaving on a twenty-two-nation tour of Europe and Africa sponsored by the State Department.

Maya's mind raced. This was the chance of a lifetime: She would travel to the greatest cities in the world, see places she had dreamed of and read about since childhood, and be with a company of distinguished black performers. How could she possibly refuse such an offer?

Maya immediately accepted Dustin's proposal and telephoned San Francisco to speak with Guy and her mother. It was not an easy task, for Maya knew that she and Guy would miss each other terribly. But she had to go.

In Montreal, Maya spent her mornings enjoying the sights and sounds of the beautiful city. In the afternoons, she rehearsed with the opera company's choreographer and pianist, working through her steps and learning the lyrics. Since she would not be performing until the group opened in Venice, Italy, she sat in the wings and watched the opera each evening.

Maya was thrilled to be a part of it all: Gershwin's music ringing through the theater, the magnificent voices, the drama as the story unfolded.

Four days later, the *Porgy and Bess* company left for Italy.

After arriving in Milan, the company boarded a bus for Venice, where the tour would begin. Along the way, the bus stopped in the charming little city of Verona, the setting of Shakespeare's *Romeo and Juliet*, for a brief afternoon rest. While the other members of the cast relaxed at a sidewalk café, Maya strolled through the narrow streets, past rows of old stone houses and balconies crammed with pots of bright red geraniums. Could she really be in Italy? As lines from *Romeo and Juliet* raced through her head, she thought of the times that she and Bailey had read the play to each other back in Stamps.

In Venice, Maya spent her free hours exploring the wonders of the great medieval city: the churches and palaces, the marketplaces, and the canals where gondolas moved gracefully through mirrored waters. Eager to learn a new language, she bought a small pocket Italian dictionary and taught herself simple phrases.

On the night of Maya's debut in the role of Ruby, the enthusiastic audience cheered as she finished her dance in the final act. Backstage, her new friends crowded around her, laughing and joking and congratulating her on her fine performance. Maya Angelou had come a long way from the dusty little town of Stamps, Arkansas. Dear old Momma would have been proud.

After Venice, the company moved on to Paris, where the opera was so well received that its engagement was extended for several months. While in Paris, Maya met many African Americans who had made the city their home, and a number of them urged her to leave the opera company. She would be a sensation in the nightclubs, they said. Maya was tempted to stay. In France, there were no lynchings or racial barriers. She wouldn't be turned away from a restaurant or a hotel because of the color of her skin. But after thinking it over, she decided to remain with the *Porgy and Bess* company.

From Paris, the group moved on to Yugoslavia and eventually to Egypt. In Cairo, Maya had the distinct feeling that she had somehow come home. The hotel manager and many of the staff were dark-skinned as she was, and she realized that she was in a country where men and women of color held positions of responsibility.

As she toured the Sphinx and the pyramids, the museums and galleries rich with the relics of an

Alex Haley (center), the author of *Roots*,
is pictured here with Maya and Levar Burton,
who acted in the television
miniseries of the book.

Maya Angelou (far right) wth composer
Margaret Bonds (far left), McHenry Boatwright (standing left),
and others. Maya had recently returned to the United States.

Maya around 1970.

Maya gives her mother,
Vivian Baxter, a hug.
MARY ELLEN MARK

After the publication of her fifth autobiographical
volume, *All God's Children Need Traveling Shoes,*
Maya continued to be in high demand for inteviews.
MARY ELLEN MARK

Maya wants to be remembered as "a good human being" rather than a poet, writer, singer, dancer, actress, producer, or director.

UPI/BETTMANN

Maya reads her poem "On the Pulse of Morning" at the inauguration of Bill Clinton.

REUTERS/BETTMANN

ancient land, Maya thought of her own great heritage, and of all the unknown ancestors who had once lived on the African continent. Others in the company shared her feelings and agreed that their experiences in Egypt had impressed them deeply.

The company completed engagements in Athens, Tel Aviv, and a number of other cities before returning to Milan, Italy, where they were to perform the first American opera ever to appear at the great La Scala Opera House. Maya and the other members of the cast were nervous. The Italians knew their opera. To rich and poor alike, opera was a part of their everyday life, and audiences were very critical of singers who missed a cue or a high note. Sometimes they even shouted a guilty singer right off the stage!

But to the joy of everyone, opening night was a fabulous success. As the curtain came down on the final act, the audience rose for a standing ovation, cheering and screaming for encores. *Porgy and Bess*—and Maya—had done it again.

The next stop on the tour was Rome. The city was lovely in the springtime, and Maya lost no time exploring the ancient ruins and visiting the sidewalk cafés. But weeks after the company's arrival, Maya received a letter from her mother in San Francisco telling her that Guy missed her and had become quite ill. Maya was heartsick at the disturbing news and immediately made plans for her departure. After a year of traveling and performing throughout Europe and North Africa, she knew that she had to leave *Porgy and Bess* and return home.

Back in San Francisco, Maya was unhappy to find Guy sickly and frail. But as the weeks went by, the little boy became stronger and his handsome face broke into a smile whenever she entered the room. Maya cooked all of Guy's favorite foods and spent hours reading to him and taking him on walks through the park. Maya promised her son that she would never leave again without him and she would take him wherever she went.

For a time, Maya stayed close to home, appearing in nightclubs in the area. When an opportunity to perform in Hawaii was offered, she agreed to go only if her son, now eleven, could come with her.

In 1957, Maya and Guy moved to New York, where the young singer found work in a small nightclub. But after touring Europe and North Africa and performing in Hawaii and throughout the West Coast, she was restless. Black Americans in the theater and in the arts were beginning to gain recognition. Lorraine Hansberry's plays were drawing crowds on Broadway, and James Baldwin's books were being read throughout the country by whites and blacks alike. Maya wanted to do something meaningful to help her people's cause, and she decided to leave the stage. Ever since her years of silence in Stamps, she had kept journals of her experiences and had filled volumes with her poetry.

Now, she would let her pen act as a voice for her people.

Maya joined a group of talented young writers in the Harlem Writers' Club. She wanted to perfect her craft so that she could speak to the needs of black Americans everywhere. Through her readings and discussions with members of the group, Maya found an opportunity to strengthen her abilities.

In the late 1950s, the civil rights movement was growing and gaining attention throughout the country. After Rosa Parks's courageous stand led to the boycott of the Montgomery, Alabama, bus system, an organization called the Southern Christian Leadership Conference (SCLC) began making significant gains in the fight for racial equality. Its leader was a young black minister named Martin Luther King Jr.

One day, Maya and her friend the comedian Godfrey Cambridge went to a large Baptist church in Harlem to hear Dr. King speak. He had just been released from jail after one of his nonviolent protests and had come to New York to raise money for the SCLC. Maya and Godfrey were inspired by Dr. King's words and talked about what they could do to help raise money.

The two wrote and produced a review, *Cabaret for Freedom*, which opened at a Greenwich Village theater and was a huge success. Maya and Godfrey donated the proceeds from the show to King's organization. Soon after that, Maya was appointed the

Northern Coordinator of the Southern Christian Leadership Conference.

At a civil rights meeting one evening, Maya was introduced to Vusumzi Make (pronounced MAH-kay), a South African freedom fighter, who had come to New York to speak to members of the United Nations about the racial injustices in his country. In South Africa, a system called apartheid separated the black majority from white people. Blacks could not hold public office or participate in the government, nor could they live in white neighborhoods or do business with whites. Black children attended inferior schools and were not allowed to go to colleges or universities. People who spoke out against the apartheid policies were thrown into jails. Many others lost their lives in the struggle for freedom.

Vusumzi Make was an important leader in the Pan-African Congress, an organization that was formed by blacks and other South Africans of color to speak out against the practices of the white minority. He had been imprisoned many times for his activities against the government and was now living in exile in Egypt because of threats against his life.

When Maya heard Vusumzi Make speak at the meeting, she was inspired by his courage and dignity. She began to see that the people of South Africa were fighting against many of the same injustices as blacks in the United States.

Maya and Vusumzi Make were immediately attracted to each other. One week after they met, they were married.

For nearly a year, Maya, Vusumzi, and Guy remained in New York. During that time, Maya took a leading role in a successful off-Broadway play by Jean Genet called *The Blacks*. Vusumzi continued his work at the United Nations and frequently traveled abroad to campaign against racial segregation.

One night, just before Maya was to leave for the theater, the telephone rang and a threatening voice on the other end of the line announced that her husband would not be coming home. When Maya asked who was calling, the voice repeated the phrase, telling her that Vusumzi Make would never be seen again.

At the theater that evening, Maya was terrified and could barely remember her lines. Where was Vusumzi? What had happened to him? When the play ended, Maya was relieved to find her husband waiting for her.

When Maya told her husband about the telephone threat, he was not surprised and said that it was an action typical of the South African police, who made regular attempts to frighten the families of freedom fighters. Knowing that the situation could become extremely dangerous, Vusumzi announced that they would leave for Egypt, where his friends would offer protection.

7

Return to Africa

When Maya and Guy arrived in Cairo, they were greeted by the sights and sounds of the ancient Arab city. Everywhere they looked, crowds of people wove in and out of streets filled with camels and goats, cars and taxis. Market stalls stood jammed against one another, and children scurried across narrow, winding alleyways where men and women in long, flowing robes moved past vendors hawking their wares. The strong scents of spices, flowers, and animal manure filled the air in a strange blending of aromas.

Vusumzi, who had flown to Cairo earlier to arrange for living quarters, greeted his wife and stepson with warm, loving arms and took them to a large, elegantly furnished apartment. Maya and Guy walked through rooms richly decorated with fine oriental rugs, antiques, and tapestries. They had never seen such wealth.

In the weeks that followed, Vusumzi introduced

44

Maya and Guy to African freedom fighters who were struggling for the independence of their nations from British and European colonial rule. They also met diplomats from the Ethiopian and Liberian embassies. Guy attended classes at an American high school in Mahdi, a suburb just outside of Cairo.

For a while, Maya was content to be in Egypt once again, free to explore the wonders of the city that had brought her such peace during her tour with *Porgy and Bess*. But soon the days lay heavily on her hands. Guy spent much of his time studying and making new friends, and Vusumzi was involved with his diplomatic work. With a cook, a housekeeper, and a gardener to take care of all the chores, Maya had nothing to do. One day, she called David Du Bois, a well-known journalist (and son of the great black scholar W. E. B. Du Bois) whom she had met in Cairo. Could he find work for her?

Maya was hired as a new associate editor of *The Arab Observer*, where her job was to cover African affairs. She was delighted with the assignment, and soon found herself going through hundreds of English-language books, newspapers, and journals, preparing for her first articles.

For more than a year, Maya continued writing for the *Observer*. Guy was excelling in his studies and had made many Arabic friends. But all was not well. Vusumzi's travels abroad were keeping him away from home much of the time, and when he returned he showed little interest in his family. Maya began to realize that her marriage to Vusumzi was failing, despite her efforts to hold it together. Soon Guy would be leaving to study at the University of Ghana. Perhaps the time had come for her to move on again.

Accra, the beautiful capital city on Ghana's southern coast, welcomed Maya and Guy like an old friend. Gentle West African breezes blew in from the sea, sending a soft rustling through the palm trees. The air was alive with the musical sounds of the country's many tribal languages, and men and women in gaily colored cottons and silks called out to one another as they went about their way.

Maya and Guy spent their first days in Accra exploring the city, with its graceful parliament buildings and open-air marketplaces thriving with activity. On a hilltop high above the city, they discovered the classic Moorish architecture of the University of Ghana, the greatest center of learning on the African continent.

As they walked about Accra, Maya and her son had the feeling that they had found their first real home. In Ghana, everyone was black.

Maya and Guy were introduced to a group of black Americans who had come to Ghana to find their African roots. Maya was excited to learn that Julian Mayfield, a young writer she had met through the Harlem Writers' Club, was also living in Accra. The future looked bright, and the sadness of the recent months in Cairo began to fade.

Then one night, as Maya was waiting for Guy to return from a picnic, she received word that he had been critically injured in a car accident. Rushing to the hospital, she found that, in addition to other injuries, Guy's neck had been broken. Maya felt the world closing in on her. The tall, handsome young son lying on a stretcher in front of her was near death, and she could do nothing but thank God that he was still breathing.

For two months, Maya stayed by Guy's bedside, knowing that the slightest cough or sneeze could paralyze him for life or kill him instantly. Then, slowly, Guy began to grow stronger, and his old sense of humor returned. The two played word games and talked of all the books Guy planned to catch up on when he could leave the hospital.

By September, Guy was well enough to begin his studies, and Maya, with the help of a new friend, had found work as an administrative assistant at the university. Life was changing for the better once again.

In 1963, Ghana, once a British colony, was celebrating its sixth year of independence. Led by an energetic young president named Kwame Nkrumah, Ghana was emerging as one of Africa's most progressive nations. For several years,

Nkrumah had been encouraging black Americans to come to Ghana to live. By the time Maya and Guy arrived, two hundred or so black Americans from throughout the United States had established their homes there.

Writers, physicians, teachers, and graduate students formed the wonderfully mixed community, and there were business people, tradesmen, and farmers. Among the group were two dentists who had attended college in America with Nkrumah. Others included W. E. B. Du Bois and Maya's friend Julian Mayfield, whose wife, Ana Livia, a physician, had attended Guy after his accident.

Soon after Guy enrolled at the university, Maya and two of her friends, Vicki Garvin and Alice Windom, decided to rent a small house together so that they could share expenses. Maya added to her modest income by working as a journalist for *The Ghanian Times*.

When Maya had a free weekend, she liked to leave the bustling city behind and drive into the countryside. On one of these trips, she stopped briefly in Cape Coast, a town that had once been a holding place for newly captured slaves who were about to be sent to America and the Carribbean. Passing the dungeons where the slaves had been imprisoned, Maya thought of her own ancestors. Had any of them been held there, she wondered, crowded body to body in the darkness, struggling against chains that cut into their hands and ankles?

She could almost hear the moans.

Maya came to Dunkwa, a gold-mining town where she had decided to stay for the night. Seeing no hotels, she stopped to ask a woman where she might find a room. The woman nodded and smiled, telling Maya to follow her. Together the two walked to a thatched house where a man welcomed her inside, all the while studying Maya's face and tall, thin frame.

Motioning to Maya to take a seat in the tiny living room, the man continued to study her. He asked Maya if she were a Ga, one of the Ghanian tribes. When Maya answered that she was not, the man questioned her about other tribes.

Finally, the villager told her that he was certain that she was a member of the great Bambara tribe of Liberia. With that, the old man announced that Maya would spend the night with a young couple who had recently married.

While Maya sat in a little yard watching the young wife prepare a thick stew over her open fire, women from the village began appearing in a steady stream, entering the hut and leaving as silently as they had come. When the stew was ready, the young woman picked up the heavy pot and invited Maya into her home. There on a table before her were eggplant and ground nut stews, fried plantains, shrimp, fishcakes, and many other generous offerings. Examining all of the lovely dishes, Maya was amazed to recognize a tradition that she remembered from her childhood in Stamps, Arkansas.

Throughout the segregated South during those years, black travelers, barred from white hotels, would seek help from black ministers in finding church members who could provide food and lodging. Then, people from the congregation would contribute food, eager to share whatever they had with the traveling guests.

Maya felt a warm sensation come over her as she thought of the neighbors who had assisted Momma in the same way. Here in Ghana, the women of Dunkwa welcomed strangers into their homes, offering them food and a safe bed just as Momma and her neighbors had provided so many years before. She relaxed and enjoyed her evening, thankful for the generosity of the villagers of Dunkwa.

On another occasion, Maya and her friends gathered at the home of Julian and Ana Livia Mayfield to meet Malcolm X, the civil rights leader who was on his way back to the United States following a religious pilgrimage to Mecca, the center of the Islamic faith. Malcolm spoke of the civil rights movement in America that was growing more powerful each day. Blacks at home and abroad must continue to support the struggle, he said. Then Malcolm told a shocked audience that he was breaking away from the Black Muslim organization, whose leader, Elijah Muhammad, preached that violence was the only way to fight against segregation. The time had come to turn away from violence, Malcolm said.

After his return to America, Malcolm X wrote to Maya and her group, describing the work he was doing in the civil rights movement. Malcolm also mentioned the threats on his life by the Black Muslims and his fears for the safety of his wife and children. In another letter, Malcolm wrote Maya about his work with the Organization of Afro-American Unity, a newly formed group championing racial harmony. Malcolm asked Maya to come back to the United States to serve as his assistant.

Maya discussed the proposal with her friends, who were quick to urge her to accept. It would not be easy leaving Ghana and the many friends she had made during her three years there. Parting from Guy would be painful, but she could not ask him to join her until he had completed his studies.

Meeting with her son, Maya was relieved to hear that he, too, felt it was important that she return to the United States to work for Malcolm and the civil rights cause. There was work for her to do, and she must go.

Shortly before Maya was to leave, a friend and his children asked her if she would enjoy visiting a part of Ghana that she had not seen. Traveling through the countryside past coconut palms and brilliant displays of flowers everywhere, Maya

51

admired the beauty and relished the peaceful atmosphere.

But as the car approached a bridge, Maya was suddenly gripped with fear.

"Stop, stop the car. Stop the car!" she ordered, and quickly opened the door and got out. Calling to the children, she told them to leave the car immediately and to walk with her across the bridge as the car, with its puzzled driver, moved slowly ahead of them.

"Why were you afraid? I have rarely seen such terror," Maya's friend asked as she returned to the car. "Have you ever heard of the Keta bridge?" he asked.[8]

Maya told her friend that she hadn't. And then the man told her that years ago, the first bridges across the Keta River had frequently collapsed when flooded by sudden storms, causing people who were traveling across in wagons or carts to be washed into the river. Many people lost their lives, and those who survived learned to leave their vehicles with a driver and walk across to safety while the vehicles followed.

Maya shuddered. Why had she been so frightened? And what had caused her sudden urge to cross the bridge on foot?

The group continued into the village of Keta to visit the marketplace before returning home. As Maya moved through the stalls, a tall woman approached her and spoke to her in Ewe, a tribal language. When Maya tried to explain that she spoke only Fanti, the woman began shouting angrily and making wild gestures. Maya took a closer look at the stranger and found that the woman bore a strong resemblance to Momma.

After a few moments, the woman's expression turned from anger to deep sadness. Placing her hands on top of her head, she began swaying from side to side and moaning softly. Then the woman quietly signaled Maya to follow her. Moving from stall to stall, the stranger introduced Maya to other women in the marketplace. Each woman reacted in the same way, placing her hands on her head and swaying to a soft moan.

Finally, Maya's friend explained that hundreds of years earlier, the village of Keta was raided many times by the slave traders. On the worst of these raids, the only people who managed to escape were some children who had hidden in the deep underbrush. The present inhabitants of Keta were the descendants of those children. Listening to the story, Maya began to understand the women's behavior. Her strong resemblance to many of the villagers had caused them to think that her ancestors must have once lived in Keta!

Had Keta once been the home of her ancestors? Had the men and women who had been among those captured in that last terrible raid been her own people? For reasons she could not explain, Maya wept.

8

Journey of the Heart

Three days after Maya came back to the United States in 1965, Malcolm X was assassinated by followers of Elijah Muhammad. Deeply saddened, Maya turned once again to her writing.

In 1968, Maya wrote and produced a ten-part series on African traditions in black American life for National Public Television. The following year, she recorded *The Poetry of Maya Angelou*. In 1970, at the urging of her good friend the writer James Baldwin and others, she published the first of her five-volume autobiographical series, *I Know Why the Caged Bird Sings*.

Maya published her first book of poetry one year later. She also tried her hand at screen-writing, becoming the first black woman in America to write a Hollywood screenplay, *Georgia, Georgia*. (She also wrote the musical score for the film.)

During the following years, Maya wrote two more volumes of her autobiography and acted as narrator, interviewer, and host for a number of African American documentaries for television and the theater. She was nominated for a Pulitzer Prize in poetry, served as Distinguished Visiting Professor at several universities, and became a trustee of the American Film Institute. More volumes of poetry followed as well as the fourth book in her continuing autobiographical series.

In 1975, President Gerald R. Ford appointed Maya to the American Revolution Bicentennial Council, and in 1977, President Jimmy Carter named her to the National Commission on the Observance of International Women's Year. That same year Maya won an Emmy nomination for her role as Kunte Kinte's grandmother in the award-winning television series *Roots*.

Maya Angelou has received several honorary degrees and many citations for her work as a human rights activist. Since 1982, she has held a lifetime appointment as Reynolds Professor of American Studies at Wake Forest University.

Maya Angelou's journey through life represents the heart and the spirit of a remarkable woman who has survived the pain of abandonment, the anguish of child abuse, and the hatred of racial intolerance. In her writings, she invites her readers to share her experiences and through them to learn the value of survival, the beauty of creativity, and the importance of hard work.

Dr. Angelou takes joy in everything she does,

whether she is working in her garden or preparing a fine meal for friends, adding to her collection of African art and sculpture, or listening to music as she reads from the work of an admired writer. She is a woman of enormous energy, wisdom, faith, and compassion. Her lifetime experiences have, in the words of one writer, "left her with a fierce dignity and the rugged beauty of a cliff that has been battered by the wind but refuses to crumble."[9] Fluent in a half-dozen languages, and beloved by readers the world over, her works have been translated into French, Spanish, Russian, and Japanese. In addition to her appointment at Wake Forest, she delivers more than one hundred lectures a year throughout the country and continues to write and produce for National Public Television, often in partnership with her son, Guy Johnson.

When asked to describe her writing, Dr. Angelou said: "I speak to the black experience, but I am always talking about the human condition, about what we can endure, dream, fail, and still survive."[10]

Chronology

1928   Maya Angelou (Marguerite Johnson) is born in St. Louis, Missouri, on April 4, the daughter of Bailey and Vivian Baxter Johnson.

1930   Maya and her brother, Bailey Jr., are sent to Stamps, Arkansas, to live with Grandmother Annie Henderson after their parents' divorce.

1935– Maya and Bailey go to St. Louis to live with
1936   Grandmother Baxter, and later with their mother, Vivian Baxter; they return to Stamps.

1940   Maya graduates with honors from the eighth grade. Maya and Bailey are sent to San Francisco to live with their mother, who has remarried and moved there.

1944   Maya graduates from high school. Son, Guy Johnson, is born.

1952   Maya marries Tosh Angelos.

1954   Following divorce from Angelos, Maya joins State Department–sponsored company of *Porgy and Bess* for twenty-two-nation tour of Europe and Africa.

1959   Maya becomes Martin Luther King Jr.'s Northern Coordinator for the Southern Christian Leadership Conference.

1960   Maya writes and produces *Cabaret for Freedom* with Godfrey Cambridge and later takes leading role in Jean Genet's *The Blacks*.

1961   Maya marries Vusumzi Make and moves to Egypt. Becomes associate editor of *The Arab Observer*.

1963   After divorce from Vusumzi Make, moves to Ghana with son, Guy, and becomes administrative assistant of the School of Music and Drama at the University of Ghana. Joins the Ghanian Broadcasting Corporation and writes for *The Ghanian Times*.

1964–   Maya becomes feature writer for the *African Review;*
1966   returns to the United States to lecture at the University of California; writes play, *The Least of These;* and appears in Jean Anouilh's *Medea* in Hollywood.

1968   Writes and narrates a ten-part series, *Maya Angelou's America: A Journey of the Heart,* for National Public Television, with son, Guy, as producer.

1970   Maya is appointed writer-in-residence at the University of Kansas. *I Know Why the Caged Bird Sings,* the first volume of her autobiography, is nominated for a National Book Award.

1971   Maya publishes first volume of poetry, *Just Give Me a Cool Drink of Water 'Fore I Diiie.* A year later, this poem was placed in nomination for a Pulitzer Prize.

1972   With *Georgia, Georgia,* Maya becomes first black woman to write a Hollywood script. Narrates several African American series for television and the theater.

1974   Maya writes second screenplay, *All Day Long.* Becomes Distinguished Visiting Professor at Wake Forest University, Wichita State University and California State University. Writes second autobiographical volume, *Gather Together in My Name*.

1975   President Gerald R. Ford appoints Maya to the American Revolution Bicentennial Council. Writes second volume of poetry, *Oh, Pray My Wings Are Gonna Fit Me Well*.

58

1976 Publishes third autobiographical volume, *Singin' and Swingin' and Gettin' Merry Like Christmas*. Receives honorary doctorate from Lawrence University. Writes play, *And Still I Rise*.

1977 President Jimmy Carter appoints Maya to the National Commission on the Observance of International Women's Year. Receives Emmy nomination for role in *Roots*.

1978 Maya publishes third book of poetry, taking the title from her play *And Still I Rise*.

1981 Maya publishes fourth autobiographical volume, *The Heart of a Woman*.

1982 Appointed Reynolds Professor of American Studies at Wake Forest University.

1983 Maya publishes fourth book of poetry, *Shaker, Why Don't You Sing?*

1986 *All God's Children Need Traveling Shoes*, the fifth in the autobiographical series, is published.

1987 *Now Sheba Sings the Song* is published in collaboration with Tom Feelings.

1993 Maya delivers the inaugural poem "On the Pulse of Morning," and publishes her collection of essays, *Wouldn't Take Nothing for My Journey Now*.

1994– Maya continues her lifetime appointment at Wake Forest University, lectures throughout the country, and writes and produces for National Public Television.

Endnotes

Chapter 1

1. Information on the inaugural events was obtained from Thomas L. Friedman, "Amid a Pageant of Diversity," *New York Times* (January 21, 1993); and Catherine S. Manegold, "An Afternoon with Maya Angelou," *New York Times* (January 20, 1993).

Chapter 2

2. For a description of the early years in Stamps, Arkansas, see Maya Angelou, *I Know Why the Caged Bird Sings* (New York: Random House, 1970), pp. 3–42. Maya gives her age as three on p. 3.
3. Maya Angelou uses the word *Negro* throughout *I Know Why the Caged Bird Sings* and in other works when describing her childhood years. In later books and in interviews, she uses *black* as well as *Afro-American*.
4. Angelou, *Wouldn't Take Nothing for My Journey Now* (New York: Random House, 1993), p. 22.
5. Angelou, *I Know Why the Caged Bird Sings*, p. 14.

Chapter 3

6. Angelou, *I Know Why the Caged Bird Sings*, p. 56.
7. Angelou, *I Know Why the Caged Bird Sings*, pp. 64–65. St. Louis in the 1930s and Grandmother Baxter's family are described in Angelou, *I Know Why the Caged Bird Sings*, pp. 49–57.

Chapter 4

All events in this chapter are from Angelou, *I Know Why the Caged Bird Sings*, pp. 74–85, 102–111, 115–120, 142–156, and 164–169; and Jeffrey M. Elliot, ed., *Conversations with Maya Angelou*, Jackson, Mississippi: University Press of Mississippi, 1989), pp. 111–113, 128, and 168.

Chapter 5

Descriptions of San Francisco, Vivian Baxter, and all other events in this chapter come from Angelou, *I Know Why the Caged Bird Sings*, pp. 170–186 and 217–246; Angelou, *Gather Together in My Name* (New York: Random House, 1974), pp. 1–2; and Elliot, ed., *Conversations with Maya Angelou*, pp. 4, 18, 69, 79, 105, and 132.

Chapter 6

For descriptions of Tos Angelos, see Elliot, ed., *Conversations with Maya Angelou*, p. 89, and Angelou, *Singin' and Swingin' and Gettin' Merry Like Christmas* (New York: Random House, 1976), pp. 15–17. Maya Angelou's tour with *Porgy and Bess*, her experiences with the Harlem Writers' Club, the SCLC, the theater, and her introduction to Vusumzi Make are described in Angelou, *The Heart of a Woman* (New York: Random House, 1974), and in Angelou, *Singin' and Swingin' and Gettin' Merry Like Christmas*. See also Elliot, ed., *Conversations with Maya Angelou*, pp. 106–107 and 189.

Chapter 7

Maya Angelou described her experiences in Egypt and Ghana in Angelou, *All God's Children Need Traveling Shoes* (New York: Random House, 1986). See also Elliot, ed., *Conversations with Maya Angelou*, pp. 22–23, 97–99, 168–169, and 199.

8. Angelou, *All God's Children Need Traveling Shoes*, p. 199.

Chapter 8

For biographical information used in this chapter, please see Joanne Braxton,"Maya Angelou," *Modern American Women Writers* (New York: Charles Scribner's Sons, 1991), pp. 1–8; Dee Birch Cameron, "A Maya Angelou Bibliography," *Bulletin of Bibliography* (Westwood, Massachusetts: F. W. Faxon, 1979) vol. 36, pp. 50–52; and Elliot, ed., *Conversations with Maya Angelou,* pp. 4, 38–40, 68–70, 126–128, 180–181, 188–190, and 218.

9. Lawrence Toppman, *The Charlotte Observer* (December 11, 1983).
10. Elliot, ed., *Conversations with Maya Angelou,* p. 158.

Chronology

For a more comprehensive Maya Angelou chronology, please see Elliot, ed., *Conversations with Maya Angelou,* pp. xiii–xvi.

Selected Bibliography

BOOKS BY MAYA ANGELOU

I Know Why the Caged Bird Sings. New York: Random House, 1970.

Maya Angelou describes her beginnings as a "tagged child," her early years in Stamps, Arkansas; St. Louis, Missouri; and San Francisco.

Gather Together in My Name. New York: Random House, 1974.

Seeking independence for herself and her fatherless child, Maya strikes out on her own in San Francisco during the pre–civil rights era of the late 1940s.

Singin' and Swingin' and Gettin' Merry Like Christmas. New York: Random House, 1976.

Maya marries and divorces Tos Angelos and joins a State Department–sponsored tour of *Porgy and Bess,* traveling throughout Europe and Africa for a year.

The Heart of a Woman. New York: Random House, 1981.

In New York, Maya returns to her writing and becomes active in the civil rights movement, eventually falling in love with and marrying Vusumzi Make, a South African freedom fighter.

All God's Children Need Traveling Shoes. New York: Random House, 1986.

Maya chronicles her life in Egypt and, later, in Ghana, as she searches for her ancestral roots.

Wouldn't Take Nothing for My Journey Now. New York: Random House, 1993.
Twenty-four essays on the importance of spirituality, compassion for others, and the power of prayer.

POETRY BY MAYA ANGELOU

Just Give Me a Cool Drink of Water 'Fore I Diiie. New York: Random House, 1971.
Maya's first published collection of poems, written with joy, sadness, and the pain of being black in a white world.

Oh, Pray My Wings Are Gonna Fit Me Well. New York: Random House, 1975.
Maya's rich and passionate voice continues to speak from the heart.

And Still I Rise. New York: Random House, 1978.
Maya's third volume focuses on courage, survival, and pride in one's people.

Shaker, Why Don't You Sing? New York: Random House, 1983.
Written with a gospel voice, a collection of remembrances of times past, shattered dreams, and the search for freedom.

On the Pulse of Morning. New York: Random House, 1993.
The inaugural poem, delivered on January 20, 1993, in celebration of a new administration. Available in hardback and in paper.

WORKS ABOUT MAYA ANGELOU

Braxton, Joanne. "Maya Angelou." *Modern American Women Writers.* New York: Charles Scribner's Sons, 1991, pp. 1–8.

Cameron, Dee Birch. "A Maya Angelou Bibliography." *Bulletin of Bibliography.* Vol. 36, pp. 50–52. Westwood, Massachusetts: F. W. Faxon, 1979.

Elliot, Jeffrey M., ed. *Conversations with Maya Angelou.* Jackson: University Press of Mississippi, 1989.

Friedman, Thomas L. "Amid a Pageant of Diversity." *New York Times,* January 21, 1993.

Manegold, Catherine S. "An Afternoon With Maya Angelou." *New York Times,* January 20, 1993.

Index

Page numbers in *italics* refer to photographs.

68